Preparing Your Company for QS-9000

Also available from ASQC Quality Press

IASG Sanctioned QS-9000 Interpretations
International Automotive Sector Group

Integrating QS-9000 with Your Automotive Quality System
D. H. Stamatis

After the Quality Audit: Closing the Loop
on the Audit Process
J. P. Russell and Terry Regel

Managing Records for ISO 9000 Compliance
Eugenia K. Brumm

The ISO 9000 Auditor's Companion and *The Audit Kit*
Kent A. Keeney

Statistical Process Control for Long and Short Runs,
Second Edition
Gary K. Griffith

Failure Mode and Effect Analysis: FMEA from Theory
to Execution
D. H. Stamatis

To request a complimentary catalog of publications,
call 800-248-1946.

Preparing Your Company for QS-9000

A Guide for the Automotive Industry

Second Edition

Richard Clements
Stanley M. Sidor
Rand E. Winters Jr.

ASQC Quality Press
Milwaukee, Wisconsin

Preparing Your Company for QS-9000: A Guide for the Automotive Industry
Second Edition
Richard Clements, Stanley M. Sidor, and Rand E. Winters Jr.

Library of Congress Cataloging-in-Publication Data
Clements, Richard Barrett, 1956–
    Preparing your company for QS-9000: a guide for the automotive
industry / Richard Clements, Stanley M. Sidor, Rand E. Winters, Jr.
— 2nd ed.
        p. cm.
    Includes bibliographical references and index.
    ISBN 0-87389-366-2
    1. Automobile industry and trade—United States—Quality control—
Standards. 2. Automobiles—Parts—Design and construction—Quality
control. 3. ISO 9000 Series Standards. I. Sidor, Stanley M.,
1957– . II. Winters, Rand E., 1944– . III. Title.
TL278.C58   1996
629.2—dc20   96-2341
                                                          CIP

10 9 8 7 6 5 4 3 2 1

ISBN 0-87389-366-2

Acquisitions Editor: Roger Holloway
Project Editor: Jeanne W. Bohn

ASQC Mission: To facilitate continuous improvement and increase customer
satisfaction by identifying, communicating, and promoting the use of quality
principles, concepts, and technologies; and thereby be recognized throughout
the world as the leading authority on, and champion for, quality.

Attention: Schools and Corporations
ASQC Quality Press books, audiotapes, videotapes, and software are available at quantity discounts with bulk purchases for business, educational, or
instructional use. For information, please contact ASQC Quality Press at
800-248-1946, or write to ASQC Quality Press, P.O. Box 3005, Milwaukee,
WI 53201-3005.

For a free copy of the ASQC Quality Press Publications Catalog, including
ASQC membership information, call 800-248-1946.

Printed in the United States of America

∞ Printed on acid-free paper

Quality Press
611 East Wisconsin Avenue
Milwaukee, Wisconsin 53202

C O N T E N T S

PREFACE

All first-tier suppliers to Ford, Chrysler, General Motors, and other participating customers have to comply with QS-9000. In addition, the second- and third-tier suppliers will soon feel pressure to comply also. This book is written for any company that needs to learn more about QS-9000. It is an introduction to the new automotive supplier quality assurance requirements (QS-9000). Here you will learn what is inside QS-9000, how ISO 9000 played an important role in its formation, who the main players are in the registration scheme, and where you can obtain further information about the standard.

In this, the second edition, we have added material to explain the 1995 revision of QS-9000. We also have included several new features.

1. A list of Internet resources related to QS-9000 and quality management

2. A new and improved checklist for QS-9000 compliance

3. A new and expanded list of qualified registrars

4. The distribution source for the officially sanctioned interpretations of QS-9000 requirements

5. A list of national bodies that now recognize QS-9000

6. The new alternative to being reaudited every three years to maintain registration

If you are the project director for implementing QS-9000, this is the first book you should read to get a grip on the requirements and what will be expected of your company. If you need to brief management on QS-9000, this book makes an excellent handout to answer many of their questions. If you are trying to convince management to adopt QS-9000, good arguments are noted within the book. If you just want a quick overview of QS-9000 so that you are informed of current developments in the supplier quality assurance field, this is the book for you.

In addition, you can use the QS-9000 checklist to audit your own company to get a initial estimate of your level of conformance. You can find the contact information for locating sanctioned interpretations, selecting a registrar, checking a registrar's qualifications, obtaining the supporting manuals for QS-9000 distributed by the Automotive Industry Action Group, and talking to other quality professional about how they are coping with QS-9000. In short, this is the one guide needed to get started with QS-9000.

ACKNOWLEDGMENTS

A book of this nature cannot be written or kept up to date without the help of many people. We would like to thank the following professionals who helped us with this revision. Specifically, Tripp Martin of Peterson Spring and the ASQC Automotive Division; Patricia Kopp, ASQC's Standards Administrator; Russ Jacobs of Chrysler; Steve Walsh of Ford Motor Company; R. Dan Reid; Wendy DeLange, membership secretary of the ISO 9000/QS-9000 Support Group; Robert Kozak of Entela QSR; Mike Zaharakos, a lead auditor for QS-9000; and the many readers who sent us e-mail offering suggestions after reading the first edition, were particularly insightful in their observations. As always, the views expressed by the authors are our own and do not necessarily reflect the opinions of the reviewers, the Automotive Task Force, or the ASQC Automotive Division.

C H A P T E R

What Is QS-9000?

Introduction

Ford Motor Company, Chrysler Motors, and General Motors Corporation, three of the world's largest automotive manufacturers, have long competed with each other. Since the late 1980s, however, these same automakers have recognized that they would gain several advantages by adopting common standards for their industry, especially for the supplier network. As an example, a measurement system analysis manual was developed in 1990 through a joint task force and is now available through the Automotive Industry Action Group (AIAG). In 1991, a statistical process control (SPC) reference manual was also developed. Now a new standard for quality assurance management systems is available. It is called *Quality System Requirements: QS-9000* and is often referred to as QS-9000.

These efforts to commonize existing practices have helped companies to develop a better understanding of topics of mutual interest within the automotive industry. There are several advantages to this approach, one being the ability of one supplier using one set of instructions to satisfy many customers.

These benefits have inspired the Big Three automakers to change their quality assurance management system requirements as well. These changes take two forms.

1. Internationalization of quality requirement standards

2. Harmonization of requirements among the automakers

Internationalization involves adopting ISO 9001 from the ISO family of standards as the basis for the new automotive supplier quality requirements. *Harmonization* results from blending the formerly separate quality system requirements of Ford, Chrysler, General Motors, and the heavy trucking industry. The resulting requirements are called QS-9000. It combines the common requirements of these major customers, the general requirements of ISO 9001, and the specific requirements of individual customers.

The goal of QS-9000 is to provide a common basis for continuous improvement, defect prevention, and variation and waste reduction, and to provide a starting point for a closer working relationship among suppliers and the customer corporations in the automotive industry.

For you, a manager at an automotive-related company, QS-9000 represents the newest change in a long history of automotive quality requirements. As before, a new requirement means you have to make new action plans for your company. This book will help you better understand the new requirements, ISO 9000, and the opportunities presented by QS-9000.

What Is QS-9000?

In June 1988, at a conference held by the Automotive Division of ASQC, the senior procurement managers of Ford, Chrysler, and General Motors were asked about the potential for developing common automotive supplier standards. The representatives from the three automotive original equipment manufacturers (OEMs) asked the ASQC Automotive Division to provide a neutral forum for such discussions. Thus, the Supplier Quality Requirement Task Force was born.

In 1990, the group released a manual for measurement system analysis. This gave automotive suppliers a common way to calibrate measurement equipment and evaluate the error present in such devices.

In 1992, a common approach to SPC was released by the task force for distribution through AIAG. Other manuals followed. Then, in December 1992, the group began to consider developing a common set of quality system requirements that combined existing programs of the Big Three automakers. At the same time, interest in ISO 9000 was growing rapidly in the United States and Canada.

A document called *Quality System Requirements (Draft)* was proposed. It combined the common elements of the previous quality system requirements of Ford, Chrysler, and General Motors. ISO 9001 was the basic set of requirements around which the document was structured; these requirements appeared in italics and additional requirements of the customer appeared in normal text. In August 1994, the official name of the document was changed to *Quality System Requirements: QS-9000.* At the end of September 1994 it was announced that QS-9000 would immediately replace all previous automotive supplier quality programs such as Ford's Q-101, General Motors' Targets for Excellence, General Motors' General Quality Standard for Europe, and Chrysler's SQA.

Several heavy truck manufacturers, such as Navistar International and PACCAR, also adopted the QS-9000 requirements. It is likely that other automotive OEMs will adopt QS-9000 in the future.

The Three Sections of QS-9000

Section 1: ISO 9000–Based Requirements. Each element is numbered from 4.1 to 4.20, just as in ISO 9001:1994. The title of each requirement is also the same. Each element begins with the exact text of that element in ISO 9001, shown in italics. Following each element is a description of additional automotive/heavy trucking requirements, shown in regular type. As such, QS-9000 Section 1 is an expansion of ISO 9001 specifically applied to the automotive industry.

Section 2: Sector-Specific Requirements. Requirements specifically for automotive suppliers that are common, but beyond the scope of ISO 9001, are noted in this section. Specifically, production part approval process, continuous improvement, and manufacturing capabilities are addressed. Most of these programs are already in place within the automotive industry.

Section 3: Customer-Specific Sections. Requirements unique to either Ford, General Motors, or Chrysler are stated in this section. Heavy trucking requirements are found in separate documents issued by each company. You must discuss with your customers which requirements will apply to any upcoming or existing contracts. These three sections comprise the bulk of the QS-9000 requirements. The document is expected to be adopted by all tier-one Chrysler suppliers worldwide by July 31, 1997, and by all tier-one General Motors suppliers by December 31, 1997. All requirements of the document must be incorporated into your company's quality system.

Appendices: Further Important Information. You should not overlook the appendices of QS-9000. For example, Appendix A provides a good description of the registration process. Appendix B is the code of practice for the registrars. You should receive this appendix as part of a quote from a registrar. It can be used to assess the registrar's compliance to the requirements. Appendix G is written for accreditation bodies, and its acceptance is the basis of Big Three recognition of them for QS-9000. It also includes requirements for registrars and auditors. Appendix H is a table of time required for registration audits to last. These represent the minimum amount of time a registrar will examine you and can be used internally for planning purposes.

QS-9000 is unique because it will introduce the characteristics of the ISO 9000 family of standards and its registration process into the automotive industry. This creates three important changes in the system. First, ISO 9001 requires that a set of written policies be created about each element within the standard. This document is called a level I document or quality manual. Second, auditing will be based on conformance to the standard and quality system effectiveness. Documentation is key for a successful audit. Third, in many cases it requires third-party registration. This requires that you pay a qualified outside organization to perform the QS-9000 audit.

If you use QS-9000 you must be aware of the IASG-sanctioned interpretations. These are the official interpretations of the QS-9000 document made by representatives from the automotive industry. They modify the requirements of QS-9000 and must be used in conjunction with that document. The sanctioned interpretations are available from ASQC and can be ordered by calling 800-248-1946 in the United States or 414-272-8575 outside the United States. The interpretations are published every few months on an irregular schedule. You should check every three months for new interpretations.

Also available from AIAG is a companion document called the *Quality System Assessment* (QSA). It describes the registration process and provides a checklist of questions to help you evaluate your level of conformance to QS-9000. The importance of this document cannot be understated. These are the questions and requirements used by registrars to construct the checklists used during QS-9000 registration audits. Therefore, you should obtain a copy of this document and study it closely along with QS-9000.

Implications of QS-9000

These changes to the quality requirement system will affect the automotive industry. The changes also may lead to rumors and overreaction. Reviewing another recent industry change demonstrates some potential effects.

QS-9000 is not the first example of a common requirement for automotive suppliers. In the 1980s, the major automotive manufacturers adopted SPC as a major quality assurance tool. Suppliers were instructed to study SPC and implement it in their plants. Although training was provided, many suppliers did not immediately comply. In addition, suppliers were confused about how to implement SPC and how SPC systems would be audited by customers. A few years into the requirement for SPC usage, the automotive makers began to contractually require SPC. Also, training became more consistent and the auditing methods for SPC compliance became more uniform. It took a few years to set the details of SPC requirements. Some mistakes were made, some consultants made lots of money, and some companies discovered they really didn't need to use SPC as much as they thought they did.

Because of this confusion, local support groups formed, trade associations created standard SPC training, and many books were written on the subject. As a result, the supplier community received ever-increasing information on how to implement an SPC system correctly and economically.

It is not unlikely that the QS-9000 implementation requirement may have a similar history. To prevent the same level of confusion, the IASG was established to issue sanctioned interpretations of the QS-9000 document and to oversee its future revisions. The Big Three automakers have provided a fax number for inquiries about QS-9000, 614-847-8556, and they have made public presentations to the supplier community to answer questions. Therefore, you should obtain copies of these sanctioned interpretations as part of your implementation effort.

Also, stay in close contact with your customers and keep informed on developments relating to QS-9000. Training and education of top managers in your company is the key to successful implementation. Managers must realize that QS-9000 is a management system model, thus they have key roles in its implementation. QS-9000 also represents an opportunity to make changes in your company that could make it more efficient and effective. The major implication is that automotive-related companies must adjust their quality assurance management systems.

Where to Start with Implementing QS-9000? Begin with ISO 9000

Some managers in automotive-related companies may be unfamiliar with or misinformed about the ISO 9000 family of standards and the ISO registration process. This is unfortunate, since the ISO 9000 family of standards is possibly the fastest growing and most dynamic topic in the quality assurance field since the introduction of statistical methods.

Let's start with some basics. In Geneva, Switzerland, is an organization called the International Organization for Standardization, or ISO. It develops and promotes international standards for trade and manufacturing.

One group of standards it has promoted successfully is the ISO 9000 series. The term *iso* is from the Greek root meaning *equal* or *equivalent.* Although it is often called ISO 9000, ISO 9000 is actually a family of standards, with three separate documents forming the contractual core. You select one of these three core standards as the model against which your company is registered.

> ISO 9001, *Quality systems—Part 1: Model for quality assurance in design, development, production, installation and servicing*
>
> ISO 9002, *Quality systems—Model for quality assurance in production, installation and servicing*
>
> ISO 9003, *Quality systems—Model for quality assurance in final inspection and test*

Most automotive suppliers will find that their business matches the requirements of most or all of the elements of ISO 9001 or ISO 9002.

In addition, a family of supporting standards exists for use as guidelines to the core standards. These guideline documents help companies mold the ISO 9000 series to fit their business. There are guidelines for software companies, project management, quality plans, how to implement specific standards, and other topics.

> ISO 8402, *Quality management and quality assurance—Vocabulary*
>
> ISO 9000-1, *Quality management and quality assurance standards—Guidelines for selection and use*

ISO 9000-2, *Quality management and quality assurance standards—Part 2: Generic guidelines for the application of ISO 9001, ISO 9002 and ISO 9003*

ISO 9000-3, *Quality management and quality assurance standards—Part 3: Guidelines for the application of ISO 9001 to the development, supply and maintenance of software*

ISO 9000-4, *Quality management and quality assurance standards—Part 4: Guide to dependability programme management*

ISO 9004-1, *Quality management and quality system elements—Part 1: Guidelines*

ISO 9004-2, *Quality management and quality system elements—Part 2: Guidelines for services*

ISO 9004-3, *Quality management and quality system elements—Part 3: Guidelines for processed materials*

ISO 9004-4, *Quality management and quality system elements—Part 4: Guidelines for quality improvement*

ISO 9004-5, *Quality management and quality system elements—Part 5: Guide to quality assurance for project management*

ISO 10005, *Quality management—Guidelines for quality plans*

ISO 10011-1, *Guidelines for auditing quality systems—Part 1: Auditing*

ISO 10011-2, *Guidelines for auditing quality systems—Part 2: Qualification criteria for auditors*

ISO 10011-3, *Guidelines for auditing quality systems—Part 3: Management of audit programmes*

ISO 10012-1, *Quality assurance requirements for measuring equipment—Part 1: Metrological confirmation system for measuring equipment*

ISO 10012-2, *Quality assurance requirements for measuring equipment—Part 2: Control of measurement processes*

ISO 10013, *Guidelines for developing quality manuals*

ISO 10014, *Guide to the economic effects of quality*

ISO 10015, *Continuing education and training guidelines*

This list is not complete; new standards are being developed continuously. Some of the newer standards are in draft international standard form. Contact the American National Standards Institute at 212-642-4900 for a complete list of the available standards or a copy of the compendium of ISO 9000–related standards.

The primary fact to remember about this family of standards is that it represents various models for a quality assurance management system. In other words, the emphasis, first and always, is on your company's management. These are *not* standards that apply only to the quality assurance department.

Each standard is developed in cooperation with participating countries, who in turn give the standard their own national designation. For example, the American National Standards Institute (ANSI) is the U.S. member body of ISO. Because ASQC is the U.S. member of ANSI responsible for quality management standards, ASQC publishes an American English version of the ISO 9000 series, called the Q9000 series. To date, more than 90 countries have adopted the ISO 9000 standards, and more than 50 of these have developed national versions.

Each of the three core standards are models for quality assurance management systems; in other words, the way in which top management organizes company-wide quality assurance efforts. The ISO 9000 family of standards was originally intended as a generic standard for customer companies to use for supplier certification; this use is called a *second-party audit*. However, the customer-driven demand for "ISO 9000" has initiated an independent third-party audit system, that is, a company needs a third-party audit so that multiple customers' requirements are met. This is increasingly true for companies engaged in international trade.

The standards also provide for expansions to be made based on a particular industry's needs. Therefore, the automotive industry's expansion of ISO 9001 covering the basic practices automotive industry quality requirements conforms with the intent of the ISO 9000 family of standards.

A driving force behind the expanding use of the standards was the European Economic Community (EEC), now called the European Union (EU). Part of the 1992 agreement to form the EEC was adopting the ISO 9000 family of standards as one of the sets of standards used to facilitate trade between participating nations. Today, more than 40,000 firms in Europe are registered to either ISO 9001, ISO 9002, or ISO 9003. Sometimes it surprises North American firms to see the ISO 9000 family of standards suddenly appear as a quality assurance requirement in customer relationships. What has happened is that many European firms have extensive business dealings in North America so they are forcing the ISO 9000 requirements onto their North American suppliers.

Many companies are also seeing ISO 9000 registration as a marketing tool. Thus, nonmanufacturing companies, banks, law firms, engineering services, and even schools are considering adopting the models presented by the ISO 9000 family of standards.

The Cast of Characters and Some Common Terms

Let's meet some of the people and processes that are part of ISO 9000 implementation. These same forces will be part of QS-9000 implementation.

The registrar—An organization that provides third-party auditing, surveillance, and registration as a service to your company and your customers. It is the registrar that audits your company and certifies you as meeting ISO 9000 and/or QS-9000 requirements. Not all registrars, however, are recognized for QS-9000 audits. A list of those registrars approved at the time of publication can be found in chapter 6, and Appendix B of the QS-9000 document details the qualifications for an approved registrar. These include being trained in a certified course on how to audit QS-9000 and being a nationally accredited registrar.

Accreditation body—The registrar should in turn be audited by a nationally recognized accreditation body. In the United States, the Registrar Accreditation Board (RAB) provides this function; in the United Kingdom, the United Kingdom Accreditation Service (UKAS); and in the Netherlands, the Dutch Certification Council (RvA).

Auditors (sometimes called assessors)—These are people that audit your company. Auditors need to receive training and pass certification exams on how to conduct ISO 9000 and QS-9000 audits. The QS-9000 training involves a sanctioned course and exam. These people are known as *certified auditors* and will have a registration number held by the registrar they represent. Anyone can be a self-proclaimed auditor, but only certified auditors are legitimate assessors of ISO 9000/QS-9000 compliance. A registrar hires certified assessors to perform audits at client companies.

Technical expert—Frequently, registrars will hire a technical expert as an addition to the audit team. The technical expert's role is to fill in missing knowledge among auditors at a specific site. For example, a chemical company may require that a chemist be part of the audit team to make auditors aware of normal processing procedures for controlling product quality.

Lead auditors (or lead assessors)—Each audit team has a leader, known as the lead auditor. The lead auditor is in charge of the on-site assessment of a company. The title *lead auditor* is certified and assigned by the registrar, meaning that the person has passed all requirements of a certified auditor and has led audits under direct supervision.

Product—This is the hardware, software, service, or processed material your company supplies. QS-9000 applies specifically to production materials, production parts or services, and finishing services such as heat treating, painting, plating, and the like.

Supplier—In the ISO 9000 family of standards, the term *supplier* means your company: the company attempting to comply to the standard. For QS-9000 it refers to the companies supplying production materials, parts, or services directly to Ford, Chrysler, General Motors, or any corporation subscribing to QS-9000.

Subcontractor—The provider of production materials, parts, or services directly to a supplier of Ford, Chrysler, General Motors, or any corporation subscribing to QS-9000.

Purchaser—In the ISO 9000 family of standards, this is another term for your customer. In the case of QS-9000, Chrysler, Ford, General Motors, and heavy trucking are among the purchasers.

First-, second-, and third-party audits—When you perform an internal quality assessment, this is a first-party audit. When your customer examines your quality system, this is a second-party audit. When an independent organization (such as a registrar) examines your company, this is a third-party audit.

Registration—Registration means that a third party (the registrar) has certified your company as meeting the requirements of ISO 9001/9002/9003, QS-9000, or both. This is the goal of a third-party audit.

Surveillance—A certified or registered company must undergo regular surveillance by a registrar to ensure that conformance is maintained. The QS-9000 document specifies that surveillance occur every six months, but this may be modified by customers. Every three years a complete reassessment audit is required.

Consultant—An outside person hired to assist your company in achieving ISO 9000 or QS-9000 standard registration. Choose a consultant carefully: to date, consultants are not registered by qualification. Refer to Appendix B in QS-9000 and the sanctioned interpretations for further guidance on selecting a consultant.

Level I, II, and III documents—The ISO 9000 family of standards uses a unique naming scheme for types of documents. Policy statements are seen as level I; standard operating procedures are seen as level II; work instructions and quality records are seen as level III.

Compliance—To conform with the requirements of QS-9000. Chrysler and General Motors require verification through a third-party audit. At this time, Ford does not require the third-party audit, but will accept it.

The Purpose of ISO 9000

Let's discuss what an ISO 9000 standard does *not* do. First, it does not guarantee product quality. In fact, product quality is not directly mentioned in the standard. Second, it is not like other supplier quality assurance requirements, in that it contains many of the same requirements, but the seriousness and objectivity of the registration procedure are different.

The purpose of ISO 9000 registration is to bring consistency and objectivity to supplier quality assurance activities. ISO 9000 standards are intended to be used between companies, usually in the customer–supplier format. The standards help companies formalize quality assurance management systems and production consistency. Continuous improvement is implied. Using independent third-party auditors has increased customers' confidence in a supplier's quality management system.

These requirements are not radical or overbearing. Instead, they reflect the basic system needed for a formal, yet minimal, quality assurance system. This is why policies, procedures, and work instructions must be documented: they must be written down so that employees follow them consistently. Once written down, they can be examined for effectiveness and be improved.

The ISO 9000 family of standards is also intended to be flexible. If your company has a unique method of operation, the standards allow for this. Exemptions and additions to the requirements are possible.

The Advantages of ISO 9000

There are three basic advantages to using the ISO 9000 family of standards. First is for the meeting of regulatory requirements. Safety- and health-related items sold in Europe are already under regulations requiring the use of the standards. More items will be added each year.

Second is for the meeting of corporate customer needs. The largest pressure for the use of ISO 9000 comes from the industrial marketplace. The standards are quickly becoming the international minimum for quality assurance. Therefore, companies should at least investigate complying with the standards. Companies should ask customers their plans for ISO 9000; several of them may be either starting to require the standard or thinking about using the standard. As QS-9000 shows, sometimes a large industrial base can adopt the ISO 9000 family of standards for wide-scale application.

Third is as a model for companies seeking to formalize their quality assurance management system. For example, ISO 9004-1 can be used by itself as a guide for total quality management.

How to Cope
with QS-9000

Your first step in preparing for QS-9000 is to confirm that you need to conform. If you have received written notification from a customer, then you need to conform. The applicability section on page 2 of the QS-9000 document should also be studied to see if you are directly affected. It reads,

> QS-9000 applies to all internal and external suppliers of: a) production materials, b) production or service parts, or c) heat treating, painting, plating or other finishing services *directly* to Chrysler, Ford, General Motors, or other OEM customers subscribing to this document.

Otherwise, talk to your customers and ask them about QS-9000 and ISO 9000. Record their reactions and comments. Repeat this exercise every few months and watch for a changing interest level in your conforming. Once you see a trend toward requiring the use of these standards, begin your implementation.

If you are an automotive parts supplier or in an automotive-related industry, then you should know about topics such as SPC, failure mode effect analysis, sample submissions, advanced quality planning, and other industry requirements. These requirements continue under QS-9000. If you previously participated in programs such as Targets for Excellence (GM), Q-101 (Ford), SQA (Chrysler), or other OEM programs, you are already familiar with these topics.

What *has* changed is that a third-party audit is possible and ISO 9001 is added to the list of requirements. As mentioned previously, both these changes are significant and affect how you cope with QS-9000.

How to Prepare Your Company

Education is the first step in preparing your company for QS-9000. Begin by training the person that will lead the implementation effort. That person should be familiar with ISO 9000 requirements and all current automotive requirements. Education can be accomplished with books, videotapes, audiotapes, and seminars. These authors recommend, as a minimum, an overview seminar, a class on documentation methods, and a course on how to perform internal audits for ISO 9001.

Once trained, the project leader can teach managers about QS-9000 and how to successfully achieve implementation. Successful implementation involves careful documentation of your quality system, complete record keeping, internal audits, and a carefully prepared implementation plan.

There are many ways to implement a quality assurance management system to meet the QS-9000 requirements. A goal of implementation should be to create a system that adds more value to the company than the money spent to implement it. A typical implementation plan might cover the following 10 steps.

1. Establish a steering committee of managers to write level I documents and oversee implementation.

2. Appoint a QS-9000 management representative to lead the implementation and to serve as the company customer liaison.

3. Conduct an baseline audit of your existing system to determine the level of action required for QS-9000 conformance.

4. Write an action plan based on management discussions and the baseline audit. Assign specific tasks to specific managers. Develop a project management timeline.

5. Revise your quality procedures manual (level II) to reflect QS-9000 requirements.

6. Select a registrar if you will undergo a third-party audit. Second-party audits will be conducted by the OEMs.

7. Upgrade or create written work instructions as needed.

8. Conduct a systemwide internal audit when you believe your quality system is in place and compare the results to these of the baseline audit. If few weaknesses are found, schedule a QS-9000 audit.

9. Prepare for the audit by reviewing all points of the quality system with managers and staff.

10. Be audited and respond with corrective actions, if needed.

If you perform well on the audit, your company is recommended for a QS-9000 registration. The audit team's lead auditor will submit a report to you and the registrar's board of governors. In the majority of cases, the board grants a registration certificate to companies found to be in compliance. With ISO 9001, ISO 9002, and ISO 9003, this happens in 70 percent of the cases.

If the audit reveals minor problems or a major nonconformance, you will have to submit a written corrective action plan to the registrar. Once the corrective actions are completed and documented, the registrar may elect to reaudit your company for compliance. You will be registered once the corrective actions are confirmed.

After registration, you face continuous surveillance, at least once every six months. If you are found out of compliance with any QS-9000 requirements, you once again have to submit a corrective action plan. If you do not, your company faces the possibility of losing its registration.

There are two schemes for continuous registration. The first involves a full registration audit every three years. This is the scheme used under ISO 9000. The second is to allow surveillance audits to address elements of QS-9000 in such depth that the entire system has been examined after three years of surveillance. In such a case, a new certificate of compliance is issued. This second scheme is unique to QS-9000, has proven quite profitable, and reduces the costs of continuous registration.

How to Prepare Your Documentation

As mentioned, there are three levels of documentation involved with QS-9000. Although no formal format is given for the style of these documents, the QSA lists the procedures that must be documented. Still, a major concern of companies conforming to QS-9000 is whether the proper documents have been created.

Let us begin by distinguishing when to use a particular document type. A policy explains *why* something is done. It should be short, simple, and to the point. Companywide quality goals are a good example of a policy statement. It is appropriate for policies to be written by senior managers.

A procedure explains *how* a process is performed. The who, what, where, when, and with which resources questions are answered in a procedure. Procedures are best written by department-level managers.

A work instruction spells out the steps required to complete a specific task. When an individual needs to perform a task as part of a process, a work instruction is used. Under QS-9000, a work instruction is required whenever the absence of such instructions would adversely affect the quality of the product. For example, as part of the corrective action procedure you may require that a follow-up report be submitted by the manager in the affected area. The instructions on how to fill out and submit that report is a work instruction. Work instructions are typically written by supervisors, technicians, or support personnel working in the affected area. Just about anyone in a company may assist in writing work instructions.

When you implement a QS-9000–based management system, you must assign the writing of particular documents to specific people. These people should be trained in proper documentation methods and use an agreed-upon format. All draft documents go through the approval process outlined in QS-9000 under "Document and Data Control." The documentation created, whether a policy, procedure, or work instruction, should not only conform to QS-9000 requirements; it should also benefit your company. As an example, the author of, say, a procedure would begin by drawing a flowchart of the process under study. The flowchart could be studied by a multifunctional team to evaluate more effective and efficient process methods. The flowchart would be modified accordingly. Then the draft procedure would be written to match the adjusted flowchart.

Each document should be clearly identified by revision number, authorization signature, document number, approval date, and department of origin. Each document should explain all relevant points with a minimal number of words. The document should be easy to read and understand by the people who are expected to use it regularly. Try giving the draft procedure or work instruction to a person unfamiliar with the operation involved and see if the person can describe what to do using only the document. This should uncover conflicting information, undocumented assumptions, or missing steps. The result will be a document that is clearly written and easy to use. In addition, the information assembled can be used to outline training program requirements.

What to Do Next: Exploiting the Benefits

Your next step should be to get a copy of the QS-9000 document and the QSA. Read them and seek assistance in further understanding the requirements. Get trained on documentation and auditing for the requirements. Then use the advice offered in this book to prepare your QS-9000 documentation.

Documentation training comes in many forms, and it can include software. You will need to have knowledge on how to write effective procedures and work instructions, as well as how to clearly communicate policies. Audit training can be short course on how to perform internal audits or week-long certified programs for lead auditors. Most companies will need a two- to three-day internal auditing course where you learn how to apply the QS-9000 requirements during an audit. Certified lead auditor training is an intense program designed for people wishing to become auditors for registrars. It involves a formal certification exam and has extensive requirements that include hands-on experience in participating in audits.

As does any change in business method, the new requirements will involve hard work but should present several opportunities. Consider the following before beginning your implementation effort.

1. QS-9000 registration for the automotive industry will also give suppliers either ISO 9001 or 9002 registration. This can be used as a marketing tool with nonautomotive customers.

2. By passing QS-9000 requirements down your own supply chain, you can promote a common quality assurance management system among companies. This creates uniformity and predictability in the industry.

3. Formalizing processes and tasks using procedures and work instructions gives an opportunity to reexamine the effectiveness of current methods and improve them accordingly.

4. Designing a companywide system for managing quality assurance gives a structure for integrating other requirements, such as environmental management regulations, health and safety requirements, and so on.

5. Requiring key managers to write policy statements for QS-9000 and approve procedures for their departments makes them familiar with the company's management system for audit time.

6. By incorporating cost-saving methods into your revised management system, you can increase company efficiency.

7. Both QS-9000 and ISO 9000 are good starting points for new management techniques such as total quality management and business process reengineering.

Where to Buy the QS-9000 Document and Other Resources

The QS-9000 document is available through the AIAG. The cost for the second edition is $7.00. You will also need the QSA, which costs $5.00. It has a detailed checklist for QS-9000 compliance and describes audit scoring. Shipping and handling is extra for any order.

Distribution for North America, South America, Australia, and Asia is handled by

AIAG
26200 Lahser Road
Suite 200
Southfield, MI 48034
Phone: 810-358-3570
Orders by phone: 810-358-3003
Fax: 810-358-3253

Distribution for Europe is handled by

Carwin Continuous Improvement
Unit 1
Trade Link
Western Ave.
West Thurrock
Grays, Essex
United Kingdom RM20 35J
Phone: 0708-861-333

AIAG also sells the Big Three manuals on advanced quality planning, SPC, measurement system assessment, production part approval process, and potential failure mode and effects analysis. These manuals can help you develop your quality assurance management system.

The ISO 9000 family of standards can be purchased through the official sales representative body in your country. ANSI is the source for the ISO version of the standards. Ask for either the specific standards you want or the complete collection (called the ISO 9000 compendium), get the current price, then send a check or purchase order or use your credit card.

ANSI
11 West 42nd Street
New York, NY 10018
Phone: 212-642-4900
Fax: 212-302-1286

ASQC sells the American English version of the ISO 9000 family of standards, called the Q9000 series, and the sanctioned interpretations of QS-9000. Electronic versions of the Q9000 standards on disk are also available.

ASQC
P.O. Box 3005
Milwaukee, WI 53201-3005
Phone: 800-248-1946 or 414-272-8575
Fax: 414-272-1734

C H A P T E R

Questions and Answers About QS-9000

Following are some sample questions and answers about QS-9000. The QS-9000 program is still maturing, so some of this information may not apply to specific situations or to later developments. Be sure to check with customers, support groups, and other sources of information for current requirements.

Will QS-9000 apply to second- and third-tier suppliers?

The current view is that it will eventually apply to all levels of suppliers worldwide. The main emphasis for 1995 through 1997, however, will be tier-one suppliers. QS-9000 calls for first-tier suppliers to develop second-tier suppliers using QS-9000.

Will I need to pay for my own audit?

If your customer requires a third-party QS-9000 certificate as part of your ongoing contracts, then yes, you will have to pay a registrar to perform the QS-9000 audit. In some cases it is expected that an automaker will perform audits, called second-party audits, at no charge to your company. If you pay for the audit, keep in mind that a 1994 survey found the average first-year ISO 9002 registration cost for a 250-employee automotive supplier to be $11,300. This was paid to a registrar for document review, initial visit, the actual audit, and all associated fees.

A QS-9000 audit will likely take longer and cost more. A 1995 survey by the National ISO 9000 Support Group found QS-9000 audits costing an average of 20 percent more than ISO 9000 audits. Consult Appendix H in the QS-9000 (as modified by the sanctioned interpretations) for estimates of the staff-days required to audit your company. If your product or production process is complex, or if you have multiple sites, then costs will be higher. Keep in mind that audits cover all shifts, so the total number of employees at your company is used to calculate audit lengths. Also consult the most recent version of Appendix H from QS-9000 for assistance in estimating the length of an audit for your company.

How do I find a qualified registrar?
The sanctioned interpretations are the only source of the official list of qualified registrars. QS-9000 qualified registrars will have signed an agreement of ethical principles with their accreditation bodies and will have auditors on staff that are certified to perform QS-9000 audits. Ask for written proof of these when interviewing prospective registrars. Some registrars will say this is pending, which means they have not yet achieved these qualifications. Also look for registrars with national recognition from the RAB, UKAS, or RvA. This ensures that any ISO 9000 certificate you might also receive will be recognized in many countries. Finally, check the background of auditors to make sure they are familiar with the automotive supply industry and its practices. A list of currently approved registrars for QS-9000 appears in chapter 6.

How do I find qualified consultants?
Ideally, a qualified consultant should be registered as an ISO 9000 auditor, be familiar with your

industry, and have already worked with a company throughout the QS-9000 registration process. Because of the newness of the QS-9000 document, however, very few people meet these qualifications. Therefore, proceed with caution when selecting a consultant. Be sure to hire someone with the skills needed to complete your implementation plan. Ask for and check references. Design a contract that specifies what is expected and defines the consulting relationship.

Does a QS-9000 certificate also count as ISO 9000 registration?

A successful QS-9000 audit automatically qualifies your company for an ISO 9001 or 9002 certificate. The QS-9000 audit covers all the points of ISO 9001 or ISO 9002. On the ISO 9000 certificate will be a notation under Scope listing your QS-9000 conformance. The ISO 9001 or ISO 9002 certificate can be used with nonautomotive customers as proof of your quality system's integrity.

How many times will I be audited?

The initial audit for QS-9000 should be recognized by many automotive customers, thus, one audit should satisfy many customers. To retain your certification, however, two surveillance audits will be performed each year unless a customer specifies otherwise. The scope of a surveillance audit depends on the size of your company and the complexity of its processes. As mentioned earlier, you have two choices on maintaining the certification. You can either submit your company to a complete re-registration audit every three years, or you can permit deeper surveillance audits that cover your complete system over a three-year period.

What is the RAB?

The RAB is a voluntary group in the United States performing recognition activities for registrars. In other words, it voluntarily accredits U.S. registrars. Normally this is a function performed by a national government agency assigned the task. The U.S. government has chosen not to assign such an agency, so a voluntary group does this. The RAB has teamed up in a cooperative agreement with the National Institute for Standards and Technology (NIST), which is affiliated with the Department of Commerce. Although this allows the market to control itself, it does not always lend itself to recognition of the accreditation by other governments. The RAB and the RvA are working together with other groups to correct this situation.

What is a "memorandum of understanding"?

A memorandum of understanding (MOU) is an agreement between two registrars, usually a U.S. registrar and a foreign registrar with national accreditation. When you qualify for a U.S. certificate, the U.S. registrar advances the results to a foreign registrar so that a co-registration takes place. That way, you can be better assured of international recognition of your company's certificate. MOUs cannot be used as a substitute for QS-9000 registrations. MOUs are not recognized under the QS-9000 registration scheme.

Can I lose my QS-9000 certificate?

Yes. If you are found by a registrar to be out of conformance and fail to take corrective action, your certificate can be revoked. Early in the development of the QS-9000, the automotive representatives discussed with registrars the idea of pulling a certificate if product quality drops noticeably; this issue has yet to be resolved. The automotive representatives still want to have the power to reject suppliers that provide nonconforming products.

Where can I get further information?

The best source of information on QS-9000 is the automotive companies and their sanctioned interpretations of the document. They should keep suppliers well-informed of expectations. AIAG is offering officially sanctioned classes on the QS-9000. If you are familiar with automotive requirements, then study the ISO 9000 materials that are available in books, tapes, and software. Check with your local section of ASQC or other such organizations for their sponsorship of local support groups. The Automotive Division of ASQC is also very active in this area.

Tables That Clarify the Relationship Between ISO 9000 and QS-9000

Table 4.1. Comparison of ISO 9001 and ISO 9004-1 elements to QS-9000, Section 1.

ISO 9001 Elements	QS-9000	Evaluation	ISO 9004-1 Elements
4.1 Management Responsibility	4.1	QS	0.1, 0.2, 4.0 to 4.3, 5.2 to 5.6, 18.3
4.2 Quality System	4.2	QS	0.1 to 0.4, 4.4, 5.0 to 5.3, 6.0, 15.2
4.3 Contract Review	4.3	IS	0.3, 5.1.2, 7.0 to 7.3
4.4 Design Control	4.4	QS	8.0 to 8.10, 16.6
4.5 Document and Data Control	4.5	QS	5.3, 11.5, 17.3
4.6 Purchasing	4.6	QS	9.0 to 9.8
4.7 Customer-Supplied Product	4.7	QS	9.7, 11.2
4.8 Product ID and Traceability	4.8	IS	11.2
4.9 Process Control	4.9	QS	10.0 to 10.4; 11.0 to 11.8, 15.7
4.10 Inspection and Testing	4.10	QS	9.7; 12.0 to 12.3
4.11 Inspection, Measuring, and Test Equipment	4.11	QS	13.0 to 13.5
4.12 Inspection and Test Status	4.12	QS	11.7
4.13 Control of Nonconforming Goods	4.13	QS	14.0
4.14 Corrective and Preventive Action	4.14	QS	13.4, 15.0
4.15 Handling, Storage, etc.	4.15	QS	10.4, 16.0
4.16 Quality Records	4.16	QS	5.3.4, 9.8, 17.0
4.17 Internal Quality Audits	4.17	QS	5.4, 5.5
4.18 Training	4.18	QS	18.0
4.19 Servicing	4.19	IS	16.4
4.20 Statistical Techniques	4.20	QS	0.4, 6.0, 20.1, 20.2

QS = Requirements are more stringent for QS-9000 in this area than for ISO
IS = ISO 90001 requirements, without additions

Note: QS-9000 has two additional sections, Sector-Specific Requirements and Customer-Specific Requirements.

Table 4.2. Important aspects of the sections of QS-9000.

Introduction	Goals / Purpose
Approach	Harmonization of Big Three automakers and heavy trucking approach to supplier quality. ISO 9001 requirements printed in italics. Additional requirements printed in normal type. Important wording defined: *shall, will,* and *must* = mandatory requirement *should* = preferred approach *typical, examples* = appropriate alternatives should be chosen *notes* = for guidance
Implementation	ISO 9000 registration may be insufficient if the requirements of this standard are not considered.
Hierarchy of Documentation	Quality system documentation progression
Section I	**ISO 9000–based requirements and automotive requirements**
Section II	**Automotive and heavy trucking specific requirements:** 1.0 Production part approval process. 1.1 Utilize Big Three requirements set forth in Production Part Approval Process Manual. It is the supplier's responsibility to determine applicability of document. 1.2 Supplier responsibility to verify changes are properly validated.
	2.0 Continuous improvement (CI) 2.1 General Comprehensive CI philosophy. Develop action plans. Note: Utilize SPC for variable data—not precontrol. Note: CI to be extended to all phases of business. 2.2 Productivity improvement—Identify and track manufacturing opportunities for CI. 2.3 Examples of continuous process improvement. 2.4 Techniques for continuous improvement. Supplier is expected to understand the use of the listed measures.
	3.0 Manufacturing capabilities 3.1 Facilities —Cross-functional team to develop facilities processes and equipment. 3.2 Mistake proofing —Utilize FMEA, capabilities studies, and others 3.3 Tool design and fabrication —Adequate resources —If subcontracted, tracking and follow-up

Table 4.2. (*continued*).

	3.4 Tool management —Maintenance capability —Storage —Setup
Section III	**Customer-Specific Requirements**
Chrysler	Appropriate use of parts identified with symbols Shield Diamond Pentagon Significant Annual layout Internal audits—one per year Design validation/production validation
Ford	Control item part Critical characteristics Setup verification Fasteners Heat treating Process and design changes Supplier modification of control items E S Test Performance QOS Material qualification Qualification sampling plans Ongoing process and product monitoring
General Motors	Publication list requirements Customer approval of control plans
Truck Manufacturers	Specific requirements—see specific manufacturer
Appendix A	Quality system assessment process Second party (customer) Third party (quality system registrar) QSA manual for self-assessments Customer decision process Flowchart of process

Appendix B	Code of practice for quality systems—registrar must be
	   accredited body
	Must include all elements
	Assessment of customer complaints and response—
	   registrar cannot provide consulting services

Appendix C	Special characteristics and symbols List of symbols and usage

Table 4.2. (*continued*).

Appendix D	Local equivalents List of standards and countries
Appendix E	Acronyms and meanings
Appendix F	Summary of changes from previous edition
Appendix G	QS-9000 accreditation body implementation requirements
Appendix H	Survey audit days table used to estimate length of registration audit Sanctioned interpretations (available from ASQC)
Glossary	Definitions of important concepts

Table 4.3. Other parts of the QS-9000 quality system.

FMEA Manual	Design FMEA Process FMEA

Production Part
Approval Process
	Submission levels for new product and changes
	Part submission warrants
	Production part approval
	    Dimensional results
	    Material test results
	    Performance test results
	Appearance approval reports

Statistical Process Control Reference Manual	Process capability studies Control charting
Measurement System Analysis Manual	Gauge R&R
Advance Product Quality Planning	Fundamentals of product quality planning Timing charts Control plans Product quality planning checklists Appendix: Feasibility commitment, DCP

C H A P T E R 5

QS-9000 Auditor's Checklist

What follows is a checklist used by a QS-9000 auditor. This does not represent an exhaustive list of questions, nor does it represent the questions you may actually be asked. Instead, it is presented to represent the types of questions to expect. In addition, you can use this information internally to evaluate your readiness for QS-9000 registration.

You can also use a copy of the QS-9000 and a copy of the QSA to create your own checklist. Both documents should be used together, since the QSA does not cover every requirement present in the QS-9000 standard. Some of these questions are based on sanctioned interpretations. Where this is the case, the interpretation reference number appears after the question in paretheses.

4.1   Management Responsibility

1. How do you ensure that your quality policy is widely known and understood?

2. Can I see your organizational chart?

3. How do you delegate authority to manage your quality system?

4. What multidisciplinary problem-solving method do you use?

5. How often do you review the effectiveness of the quality management system?

6. Can I see those meeting notes?

7. How do you ensure that qualified people are in support positions?

8. Who is responsible for QS-9000 implementation?

9. Can I see how you track, update, and monitor your business plan?

10. Is the business plan a controlled document? (9503-C11)

11. Do you use benchmarking for quality, production, and operation efficiency?

12. Can I see the data?

13. How do you measure customer satisfaction? Is it a formal plan?

14. Do you use multifunctional teams for advanced quality planning?

15. Does the company have a level I quality manual with the responsibilities included? (9508-C22)

4.2   Quality System

1. Show me your level II documentation. (Auditor examines the material to ensure that all document requirements of QS-9000 as shown in the standard have been addressed.)

2. Does the quality planning process parallel the level II document description and level III procedures for the following?

   a. Product program plan preparation

   b. Resource acquisition

   c. Design and process capability studies

    d. Updating and maintenance of quality control and inspection methods

    e. Control plan development

    f. Review of standards and specifications

3. Do you conduct design feasibility reviews? Can I see the results for products *x, y,* and *z*?

4. Did this design review also encompass statistical capabilities?

5. To what level do you develop control plans? Do the control plans cover all three phases of production, including prototyping? (9509-C23)

6. Do the control plans include all special characteristics? How do you know they do?

7. When do you revise a control plan?

8. Do control plans cover all three phases of production?

9. Do FMEAs consider special characteristics?

10. Do you develop control plans using the guidance given in *APQP Manual & Control Plans*?

4.3   Contract Review

1. How do you define a contract?

2. Is it in writing?

3. Do you require QS-9000 compliance of your subcontractors?

4. Can I see where you acquire compliance (how notified)?

5. How do you change customer requirements under a current contract when requested to do so by a customer?

6. How are contracts reviewed?

7. Can I see those records?

4.4 Design Control

1. Who is responsible for product design? How are design plans established?

2. How do you know that people assigned to a project have the necessary skills?

3. What are applicable regulation standards? How are they identified?

4. Do you use CAD/CAE? If you subcontract, how did you select the suppliers?

5. Can I see records of project/product design reviews?

6. Can those design outputs be verified?

7. Does the design output meet customers' input requirements?

8. How do you cross-reference?

9. Does your design output process include any of the following?

   a. GDT and other design techniques as listed in 4.4.2

   b. Customer performance risk trade-off analysis

      c. Testing—production and field

      d. Design FMEA

10. Can I see your performance testing results?

11. Can I see your prototype program results?

12. Do you validate designs as part of the quality planning process?

13. Can I see your engineering change procedure?

14. Show me how the engineering change notice accommodates customer-initiated change.

15. Do you have a two-way CAD/CAE interface with your customer? (9509-C35)

4.5 Document Control

1. Show me a master list of controlled documents.

2. Show me how customer-initiated changes are controlled.

3. Can I see all your reference documents?

4. Describe your document control process to me.

5. How do you control documents resident in software?

6. Are customer-special characteristics properly annotated on your documentation? (9509-C29)

7. Do you have a procedure for controlling customer engineering specifications?

4.6   Purchasing

1. Do your subcontractors meet the same standards you do?

2. How do you survey subcontractors?

3. Can I see those records?

4. Can I see a copy of your approved vendor list?

5. How do you unapprove a vendor?

6. How do you decide to monitor a vendor?

7. Are you developing subcontractors to the requirements of QS-9000?

8. Can you verify quality on site?

9. Can you show me purchase orders? (Auditor uses this question to evaluate completeness of purchasing requirements section.)

10. Is supplier on-time delivery being monitored and tracked?

4.7   Customer-Supplied Product

1. Do you inspect product supplied by your customer at receiving and then periodically to ensure its condition?

2. Show me the procedure you use.

4.8   Product Identification and Traceability

1. How do you identify product at each production stage?

2. Show me how I could take product *x* from shipping and trace it backward through the production stream.

3. Do your customers require part or component traceability?

4. Show me how you maintain traceability.

4.9   Process Control

1. How do you develop job instructions? Are such work instructions available at the work sites?

2. Are they complete with respect to accessibility, full communication of requirements, required tooling and gauges, SPC, and all the other requirements of 4.9.1?

3. Can we follow three or four jobs on the shop floor to ensure process control?

4. Do you have a preventive maintenance and predicted maintenance plan?

5. What process do you use to ensure that all regulatory safeguards are followed? Are there certificates? Can I see them?

6. What are your process controls for items designated as appearance items?

4.10 Inspection and Testing

1. How do you control purchased material?

2. Do you require that your subcontractors send you statistical data?

3. Can I see it?

4. Describe your defect prevention methods.

5. Can I follow products x, y, and z through your production process to verify your documented inspection?

6. How do you verify that product will not ship until all inspection and test procedures are complete?

7. Show me your layout and functional test records.

8. Are records maintained for the production cycle plus one year?

9. If a subcontractor is providing any final operations, is that subcontractor using your control plan? (9508-C17)

4.11 Inspection, Measuring, and Test Equipment

1. Do you use the measurement system analysis (MSA) manual guidelines to determine accuracy/precision?

2. Is the MSA noted on the control plan?

3. Do you use an outside calibration service?

4. Is the appropriate calibration standard noted on the proper outside services?

5. How is each piece of inspection, measurement, and test equipment identified?

6. How do you control or calibrate employee-acquired equipment?

7. If you drop a pair of calipers, what do you do?

8. How do you know how to use those micrometers?

9. Do you recalibrate after engineering changes?

10. How and where do you store calibration standards?

11. How can you use a gauge if the calibration sticker is missing?

12. How do you identify inspection and test status throughout the production process?

4.12 Inspection and Test Status

1. How do people on the line know the product they receive has been properly inspected or tested?

2. How do you mark the inspection and test status on your production parts?

3. May I randomly sample such parts to confirm this?

4. Are you required to have early launch controls or other identification requirements by your customer?

4.13 Control of Nonconforming Product

1. Do you have segregated hold areas?

2. Do you have a material review board (MRB) or related procedure?

3. Can I see the last six months' MRB history?

4. What are suspect products?

5. How do you control those?

6. What do you do with nonconforming and suspect parts?

7. Do you research parts?

8. How do you trace customer-approved deviations?

9. Do you record nonconformances? How?

10. Do you reinspect reworked product?

11. Show me some rework and repair instructions.

12. Do you maintain records of customer-approved deviations and authorized quantities?

4.14 Corrective Action

1. What problem-solving method do you use?

2. Do you verify corrective action effectiveness?

3. What do you feel are appropriate corrective actions?

4. Do you analyze returned parts to develop corrective actions?

5. Do you use nonconformance reports to develop corrective actions?

6. Is upper management part of the review process?

7. Show me.

4.15 Handling, Storage, and so on

1. Do you check or rotate stock?

2. Show me your packaging procedures.

3. Do you have customer packaging specifications? Can I see them?

4. Do you have a target of 100 percent on-time delivery?

5. What do you do when product is damaged in the plant?

6. Are material handling methods appropriate for the product?

4.16 Quality Records

1. Show me copies of your subcontractor development records.

2. Are records accessible on site?

3. How do you prevent deterioration of electronic records?

4. Are records retained for the following time periods at a minimum?

   a. Production plus one year

   b. Charts and other level IV documents one year

5. Are your records disposed of at the end of their retention period?

4.17 Internal Quality Audits

1. Show me the last six months' internal audit reports.

2. Are corrective actions initiated from internal audits?

3. Are auditors independent from the department/function being audited?

4. How do you schedule and prioritize audits?

5. Is upper management part of the review process?

4.18 Training

1. How did employees receive qualification/training in the aspects of their jobs?

2. Is training effectiveness verified?

3. Do you perform a training needs analysis?

4. If supervisors are qualified to approve training, how or where did they become qualified?

5. Can I see your training records?

6. How did you learn to set up this machine?

7. How did you learn to assemble this job?

4.19 Servicing

1. Show me your service reports, internal and field, for the last six months.

2. Tell me how service data are communicated to other levels of the organization.

4.20 Statistical Techniques

1. What do you do when the dots on the chart are above or below the control limits?

2. What do you do when the line is trending up or down?

3. Does advanced quality planning develop the appropriate statistical techniques?

4. Are special techniques established and used per the guidelines of the SPC manual?

Production Part Approval Process (PPAP)

1. Is the first-piece paperwork complete?

2. Are you using the PPAP manual?

Continuous Improvement

1. Does upper management have a continuous improvement philosophy? Is it implemented?

2. Are continuous improvement projects ongoing? May I see a few examples of their activities?

3. Are the basic continuous improvement techniques implemented? Is there adequate training on these techniques?

Manufacturing Capabilities

1. Is the development of new plants and processes done with cross-functional teams?

2. Is the development of new tooling tracked for completion?

3. Is tooling storage managed actively? Are setup instructions available?

C H A P T E R 6

Sources of
Additional
Information

The information provided can help you to secure further information about the QS-9000 standard.

Customer Representatives for QS-9000

Ford Motor Company
   Steve Walsh
   Ford Motor Company
   Box 1517-A, NAAO
   Dearborn, MI 48121

Chrysler Motors
   Russell M. Jacobs
   CIMS: 484-08-02
   800 Chrysler Drive East
   Auburn Hills, MI 48236-2757

General Motors Corporation
   R. Dan Reid
   General Motors Powertrain Group
   M/C 2R29
   895 S. Joslyn Ave.
   Pontiac, MI 48340-2920

Finding a QS-9000 Registrar

As of December 1995, the registrars in North America approved to conduct QS-9000 registration include the following. You should consult the most recent edition of the sanctioned interpretations, available from ASQC at 800-248-1946, to obtain a current list. Note that UKAS is the former NACCB and RvA is the former RvC.

RvA Approved
> BSi Quality Assurance
> Tysons Corner
> 8000 Towers Crescent Drive, Suite 1350
> Vienna, VA 22182
> Phone: 703-760-7828
> Fax: 703-761-2770

> BVQI (Netherlands)
> North American Central Offices
> 509 North Main Street
> Jamestown, NY 14701
> Phone: 716-484-9002
> Fax: 716-484-9003

> DNVI (Netherlands)
> Det Norsk Veritas Certification, Inc.
> 16340 Park Ten Place
> Suite 100
> Houston, TX 77084
> Phone: 713-579-9003
> Fax: 713-579-1360

> Lloyd's Register Quality Assurance
> Norfolk House
> Wellesley Road
> Croydon, CR9 2DT
> United Kingdom
> Phone: 01-81-688-6882
> Fax: 01-81-681-8146

NSF International
P.O. Box 130140
Ann Arbor, MI 48113-0140
Phone: 313-769-6728
Fax: 313-769-0109

QMI
Mississauga Executive Centre
Suite 800
2 Robert Speck Parkway
Mississauga, Ontario L4Z 1H8
Canada
Phone: 905-272-3920
Fax: 905-272-8503

Both RvA and UKAS approved
BSi Quality Assurance
P.O. Box 375
Milton Keynes MK14 6LL
United Kingdom
Phone: 44-908-220908
Fax: 44-908-231826

Both RvA and RAB approved
ABS Quality Evaluations
ABS Plaza
16855 Northchase Dr.
Houston, TX 77060-6008
Phone: 713-873-9400
Fax: 713-874-9564

Entela QSRD
3033 Madison SE
Grand Rapids, MI 49548
Phone: 616-247-0515
Fax: 616-247-7527

Intertek Services Corporation
9900 Main Street
Suite 500
Fairfax, VA 22031
Phone: 703-ISO-9000 x. 3011
Fax: 703-273-2895

KPMG Quality Registrar
150 John F. Kennedy Parkway
Short Hills, NJ 07078-2778
Phone: 800-716-5595
Fax: 201-912-6050

Quality Systems Registrars, Inc.
13873 Park Center Raod
Suite 217
Herndon, VA 22071-3279
Phone: 703-478-0241
Fax: 703-478-0645

Steel Related Industries Quality System Registrar
2000 Corporate Drive
Suite 450
Wexford, PA 15090
Phone: 412-935-2844
Fax: 412-935-6825

TUV Rheinland of North America
12 Commerce Road
Newton, CT 06470
Phone: 203-426-0888
Fax: 203-270-8883

Underwriter's Laboratory
1285 Walt Whitman Road
Melville, NY 11747-3081
Phone: 516-271-6200
Fax: 516-271-6223

RAB approved

AGA Quality
1425 Grand Vista Avenue
Los Angeles, CA 90023
Phone: 213-261-8161
Fax: 213-261-3369

American Quality Assessors
1200 Main Street
Suite M107
Columbia, SC 29201
Phone: 803-779-8150
Fax: 803-779-8109

AT&T Quality Registrars
650 Liberty Avenue
Union, NJ 07083
Phone: 800-550-9001
Fax: 908-851-3360

BVQI
North American Central Offices
509 North Main Street
Jamestown, NY 14701
Phone: 716-484-9002
Fax: 716-484-9003

Det Norsk Veritas Certification, Inc.
16340 Park Ten Place
Suite 100
Houston, TX 77084
Phone: 713-579-9003
Fax: 713-579-1360

Lloyd's Register Quality Assurance
33-41 Newark Street
Hoboken, NJ 07030
Phone: 201-963-1111
Fax: 201-963-3289

OMNEX
880 South Grove
Ypsilanti, MI 48198
Phone: 313-480-9940
Fax: 313-480-9941

SGS International Certification Services Canada Inc.
90 Gough Rd
Unit 4
Markham, Ontario L3R 5V5
Canada
Phone: 905-479-1160
Fax: 905-479-9452

TUV Essen
1032 Elwell Ct
Suite 222
Palo Alto, CA 94303
Phone: 415-961-0521
Fax: 415-961-9119

UKAS approval

NQA (Wales and Southwest England)
The QED Centre
Treforest Industial Estate
Pontypridd, CF37 5YR
United Kingdom
Phone: 01-44-384-4321
Fax: 01-44-384-4345

Smithers Quality Assessment Inc
425 West Market Street
Akron, OH 44303-2099
Phone: 216-762-4231
Fax: 216-762-7447

Any of the registrars just listed should be able to answer questions regarding registration and pricing.

The sanctioned interpretations are available from

ASQC
611 East Wisconsin Avenue
P.O. Box 3005
Milwaukee, WI 53201-3005
Phone: 800-248-1946 or 414-272-8575
Fax: 414-272-1734
Home page: http://www.asqc.org

Another source of information on QS-9000 is

ISO 9000/QS-9000 Support Group
9864 Cherry Valley
Suite C
Caledonia, MI 49316
Phone/Fax: 616-891-9114
BBS: 616-891-9433
Internet e-mail: isogroup@cris.com
Home page: http://www.cris.com/~isogroup/

The support group also provides tutorials, technical support, a monthly newsletter, and computer bulletin board discussions of QS-9000, ISO 9000, and ISO 14000.

Sanctioned National Accreditation Bodies

Ford, Chrysler, and General Motors regularly recognize national accreditation bodies. This allows the national bodies to approve registrars to conduct QS-9000 registrations. As of 1996 the list included the following bodies. These national accreditation bodies are very active in the QS-9000 area. They also publish lists of approved registrars for QS-9000 and ISO 9000.

Registrar Accreditation Board (RAB)
Registrar Accreditation Board
611 East Wisconsin Avenue
P.O. Box 3005
Milwaukee, WI 53201-3005
Phone: 800-248-1946 or 414-272-8575
Fax: 414-765-8661

RvA (Dutch Certification Council)
Raad voor Accreditatie
Radboudwwartier 223
Postbus 2768
3500 GT Ufrecht
Netherlands
Phone: 31-30-239-45-00
Fax: 31-30-239-45-39

UKAS
UKAS
Audley House
13 Palace Street
London SW1E 58HS
United Kingdom
Phone: 44-171-233-7111
Fax: 44-171-233-5115

Standard Council of Canada (SCC)
Standard Council of Canada
45 O'Connor Street
Suite 1200
Ottawa, Ontario K1P 6N7
Canada
Phone: 613-238-3222
Fax: 613-995-4564

FINAS (Finland)
FINAS
P.O. Box 239
00181 Helsinki
Finland
Phone: 358-061-671
Fax: 358-0616-7467

SINCERT (Italy)
    SINCERT
    Via Battistotti
    Sassi 11
    20133 Milano
    Italy
    Phone: 39-271-9202
    Fax: 39-271-9055

SWEDAC (Sweden)
    SWEDAC
    P.O. Box 878
    SE-501 15
    Boras, Sweden
    Phone: 46-33-177-745
    FAX: 46-33-101-392

TGA (Germany)
    Tragergemeinschaft Fur Akkrediterung GMBH
    Buro: Stresemannallee 13
    60596 Frankfurt am Main
    Germany
    Phone: 49-69-630-2380
    Fax: 49-69-630-2365

SAS (Swiss Accreditation Service)
    SAS
    CH-3084 Wabern
    Lindenweg 50
    Switzerland
    Phone: 41-31-963-3111
    Fax: 41-31-963-3210

ENAC (Entidad Nacional de Acreditacion)
CL, Serrano, 240–7th Floor
Madrid, 28012
Spain
Phone: 34-1457-3289
Fax: 34-1458-6280

JAB (Japan)
Japan Accreditation Board
Alaska Royal Building Annex
6-18 Alasaka 7 Chrome, Minato-ku
Tokyo 107
Japan
Phone: 81-3556-10375
Fax: 81-3556-10376

NMAS (Norway)
Justevesenet—Norwegian Metrology &
    Accreditation Service
P.O. Box 6832 St. Olavs Plass
N-1030 Oslo
Norway
Phone: 47-22-200226
Fax: 47-22-207772

Internet Sources

Using an Internet account and a computer modem, you can access many sources of information to help you to understand and implement QS-9000. Sending e-mail with the messages indicated will subscribe you to a mailing list where ongoing discussions of specific topics are automatically sent to you each week. Send a HELP command in the body of your message to receive additional information on how these services work.

listserv@msu.edu

> Best practices in manufacturing. Send SUBSCRIBE MFG-INFO [first name] [last name]

listserv@pucc.princeton.edu

> TQM in manufacturing and services. Send REVIEW QUALITY

listserv@ukanvm.cc.ukans.edu

> Quality improvement team leaders and facilitators. Send REVIEW TEAMS-L

listserv@vm1.nodak.edu

> ISO 9000/QS-9000 discussion. Send INFO ISO9000

listserv@vm1.nodak.edu

> Discussion of quality and environmental management systems. Send SUB QUEST [first name] [last name]

The World Wide Web is the fastest growing portion of the Internet. You use a web browser from your computer service or a separate program, such as Netscape or Mosaic, to travel the web. Also of interest are the home pages on the web where hypertext links allow you to pull up further information on a particular topic or to jump from one site to another. Try the following:

http://www.quality.co.uk/quality/certbody.htm

> List of registrars around the world.

http://138.81.2.245/9000e/forum.html
ISO 9000 forum home page.

http://deming.eng.clemson.edu
TQM and quality discussions. Some ISO 9000 material.

http://quality.org/pub/qc
Large collection of quality control and ISO 9000 information.

http://stdsbss.ieee.org
Institute of Electrical and Electronics Engineers site for standards.

http://vaxmsx.babson.edu
Babson College's web page for quality-related files.

http://vector.casti.com/qc
Quality Resources Online. Source of information on local ASQC sections online and agile manufacturing.

http://www.ansi.org
Home page of the American National Standards Institute, source of many ISO standards for use in the United States and national quality standards.

http://www.apqc.org
Home page for the American Productivity & Quality Center.

http://www.asqc.org
Home page of ASQC.

http://www.aztec.com/aztec/iso9000
ISO 9000 information.

http://www.benchnet.com
Home page for the Benchmark Exchange, a fee-based resource.

http://www.cc.emory.edu/ITD/tqm.html
Emory University's TQM web site.

http://www.creacon.com
Newsletter on quality issues.

http://www.cris.com/~isogroup/
Home page of the ISO 9000/QS-9000 Support Group.

http://www.exit109.com
ISO 9000 information.

http://www.hci.com.au/management/
Discussion of management, quality, and ISO 9000.

http://www.industry.net
Home page for the Association for Manufacturing Excellence.

http://www.iso.ch/welcome.html
ISO headquarters in Geneva, Switzerland.

http://www.netview.com/qualinet
Discussions for quality professionals.

http://www.netview.com/qualinet/
Qualinet's home page.

http://www.nist.gov
Home page for the National Institute for Standards and Technology in the United States.

http://www.nist.gov.8102/
The quality program at NIST.

http://www.ornl.gov/orcmt/
> Results of the Navy's best manufacturing practices survey.

http://www.quality.org/qc
> Quality Resources Online.

http://www.sei.cmu.edu
> Software Engineering Institute's web page.

http://www.xnet.com/~creacon/Q4Q
> Extensive source of quality information and links to other groups.

SUGGESTED READING

Brumm, Eugenia K. 1995. *Managing Records for ISO 9000 Compliance.* Milwaukee: ASQC Quality Press.

Clements, Richard. 1994. *Quality Manager's Complete Guide to ISO 9000.* Englewood Cliffs, N.J.: Prentice Hall.

Keeney, Kent A. 1995. *The Audit Kit.* Milwaukee: ASQC Quality Press.

Lamprecht, James L. 1993. *Implementing the ISO 9000 Series.* New York: Marcel Dekker.

Lamprecht, James L. 1992. *ISO 9000: Preparing for Registration.* Milwaukee: ASQC Quality Press.

Peach, Robert W., ed. 1995. *The ISO 9000 Handbook.* 2nd ed. Fairfax, Va.: CEEM Information Services.

Sayle, Allan J. 1988. *Management Audits: The Assessment of Quality Management Systems.* 2nd ed. Hampshire, U.K.: Allan J. Sayle Ltd.

Sayle, Allan J. 1991. *Meeting ISO 9000 in a TQM World.* Hampshire, U.K.: Allan J. Sayle Ltd.

Stamatis, D. H. 1995. *Integrating QS-9000 with Your Automotive Quality System.* Milwaukee: ASQC Quality Press.

INDEX

About the Authors

Richard Clements is the founder and chairman of the ISO 9000/QS-9000 Support Group, which provides information, tutorials, technical support, monthly newsletters, and computer bulletin board discussions of QS-9000, ISO 9000, and ISO 14000. He is also the president of Solution Specialists and has served as a professor at Grand Rapids (Michigan) Community College. Clements holds a master's degree from the University of Chicago and is the author of several books, including *The Quality Manager's Complete Guide to ISO 9000, The Complete Guide to ISO 14000,* and *Handbook of Statistical Methods in Manufacturing.* He also serves as a series editor of books related to international standards published by Simon & Schuster.

Stanley M. Sidor has been an industrial engineer, trainer, and plant manager since 1980. He has worked with several Michigan-based automotive, furniture, and electronic suppliers. He holds a master's degree from Western Michigan University and has served as a professor at Northwestern Michigan College and Ferris State University. He has coauthored a CAM tutorial and is a senior member of the American Institute of Industrial Engineers and the Society of Manufacturing Engineers. He holds credentials as an RAB and IQA lead auditor.

Rand E. Winters Jr., president of Rand E. Winters Group, Inc., has been a quality control manager, production manager, and plant manager for several Michigan manufacturing firms. He has a bachelor's degree in industrial engineering and a master's degree in industrial technology from Western Michigan University. Winters is on the national training staff of ASQC, SME, and the Metal Treating Institute. He is registered as a QS-9000 auditor and is a lead auditor with American Quality Assessors, a national ISO 9000/QS-9000 registration company based in South Carolina.